The English language has a rich heritage of traditional rhymes, some with music, some without. Such rhymes serve many purposes: those in the first section of this book, for example, can be used to teach co-ordination to very young children, which is now known to be important to their later development. The rhymes you will find here have been assembled to form a strong teaching sequence by age: from co-ordination and practice in numbers, memory and pronunciation to the teaching of a combination of sound, action and words. A wider selection of rhymes following this significant sequence is to be found in our standard format series Learning with Traditional Rhymes, *Books 1 – 6.*

CONTENTS

Page

Finger Rhymes

2 Round and round the garden
5 This little pig went to market
6 There were two blackbirds
9 Pat-a-cake, pat-a-cake
10 Incy wincy spider
13 Five currant buns in a baker's shop
14 My mother said that if I should

Number Rhymes

16 One, two, kittens that mew
18 One, two, buckle my shoe
20 Seven black friars, sitting back to back
22 Knock, knock, knock, knock
24 There were two wrens upon a tree
26 One, two, three, four, five
28 One man went to mow

Memory Rhymes

30 Thirty days hath September
31 Monday's child is fair of face

Page

32 A was an apple pie
34 Solomon Grundy
36 A, B, C, D, E, F, G

Talking Rhymes

38 Anna Elise, she jumped with surprise
40 My dame hath a lame tame crane
42 Peter Piper picked a peck of pickled pepper
44 Thomas a Tattamus took two T's
46 Doctor Foster went to Gloucester

Action Rhymes

48 Old McDonald had a farm
50 Sing a song of sixpence
54 I had a little nut-tree

Dancing Rhymes

56 O, have you seen the muffin man

0 7214 7513 2

The LADYBIRD book of RHYMES

by DOROTHY *and* JOHN TAYLOR

with illustrations by

BRIAN PRICE THOMAS

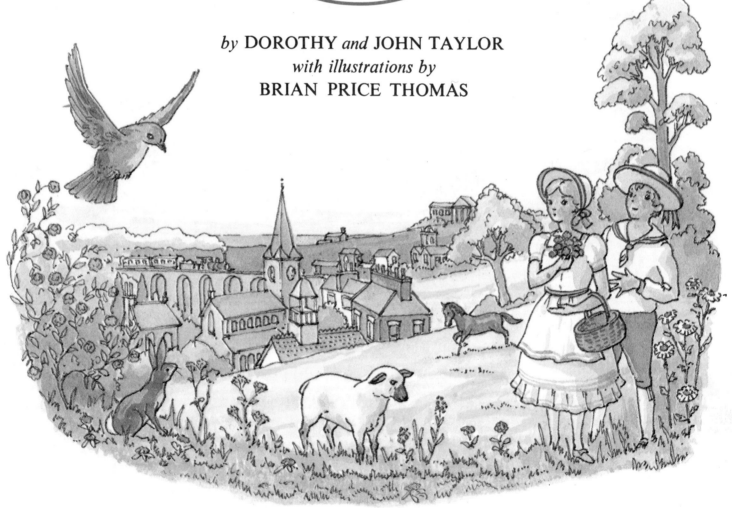

Ladybird Books Loughborough

Round and round the garden
Like a teddy bear;
One step, two step,
Tickle you under there.

This little pig went to market,
This little pig stayed at home,
This little pig had roast beef,
This little pig had none,
And this little pig cried:
Wee-wee-wee,
I can't find my way home.

There were two blackbirds
Sitting on a hill,
The one named Jack,
The other named Jill.

Fly away, Jack!
Fly away, Jill!
Come again, Jack!
Come again, Jill!

Pat-a-cake, pat-a-cake,
Baker's man,
Bake me a cake
As fast as you can.
Pat it and prick it
And mark it with 'B'
And put it in the oven
For Baby and me.

Incy wincy spider,
Climbing up the spout,
Down came the rain,
And washed the spider out.

Out came the sunshine,
Dried up all the rain,
Incy wincy spider,
Climbed the spout again.

10

Five currant buns in a baker's shop,
Round and fat with sugar on the top.
Along came a boy with a penny one day,
Bought a currant bun and took it away.

My mother said that if I should
Play with the gipsies in the wood,
She would say, 'You naughty girl!
You naughty girl to disobey!'

One, two, kittens that mew,
Two, three, birds on a tree,
Three, four, shells on the shore,
Four, five, bees from the hive,
Five, six, the cow that licks,
Six, seven, rooks in the heaven,
Seven, eight, sheep at the gate,
Eight, nine, clothes on a line,
Nine, ten, the little black hen.

1, 2,
Buckle
my
shoe;

3, 4,
Knock
at the door;

5, 6,
Pick up sticks;

7, 8,
Lay them
straight;

9, 10,
A big fat hen;

11, 12,
Dig and delve;

13, 14,
Maids a-courting;

15, 16,
Maids in the kitchen;

17, 18,
Maids in waiting;

19, 20,
My plate's empty.

Seven black friars, sitting back to back,
Fished from the bridge for a pike or a jack.
The first caught a tiddler,
The second caught a crab,
The third caught a winkle,
The fourth caught a dab,
The fifth caught a tadpole,
The sixth caught an eel,
The seventh one caught an old cart-wheel.

21

Knock, knock, knock, knock –
Hear the knockings four!
Each a knock for someone standing
At our kitchen door.

The first is a beggar man,
The second is a thief,
The third is a pirate,
And the fourth a robber chief.

Close all the windows,
Lock the door, and then
Call for the policeman quick
To catch those four bad men!

There were two wrens upon a tree,
Whistle and I'll come to thee,
Another came and there were three,
Whistle and I'll come to thee;
Another came, and there were four,
You needn't whistle any more,
For being frightened, off they flew,
And there are none to show to you.

One, two, three, four, five,
Once I caught a fish alive.
Six, seven, eight, nine, ten,
Then I let it go again.

Why did you let it go?
Because it bit my finger so.
Which finger did it bite?
This little finger on the right.

One man went to mow,
Went to mow a meadow,
One man and his dog,
Went to mow a meadow.

Two men went to mow,
Went to mow a meadow,
Two men, one man and his dog,
Went to mow a meadow.

Three men went to mow,

Four men went to mow,

Five men, *etc.*

One man went to mow, Went to mow a mea-dow,
One man and his dog, Went to mow a mea-dow.

February

April June
September November

January March May
July August October
December

Thirty days hath September,
April, June and November;
All the rest have thirty one,
Excepting February alone,
And that has twenty eight days clear
And twenty nine in each leap year.

Monday's child is fair of face,
Tuesday's child is full of grace,
Wednesday's child is full of woe,
Thursday's child has far to go,
Friday's child is loving and giving,
Saturday's child works hard for a living,
And the child that is born on the Sabbath day
Is bonny and blithe, and good and gay.

A was an Apple pie, B Bit it, C Cut it,
D Dealt it, E Eat it, F Fought for it,
G Got it, H Had it, I Inspected it,
J Joined for it, K Kept it, L Longed for it,
M Mourned for it, N Nodded at it,
O Opened it, P Peeped in it,
Q Quartered it, R Ran for it, S Stole it,
T Took it, U Upset it, V Viewed it,
W Wanted it,
XYZ All wished for a piece in hand.

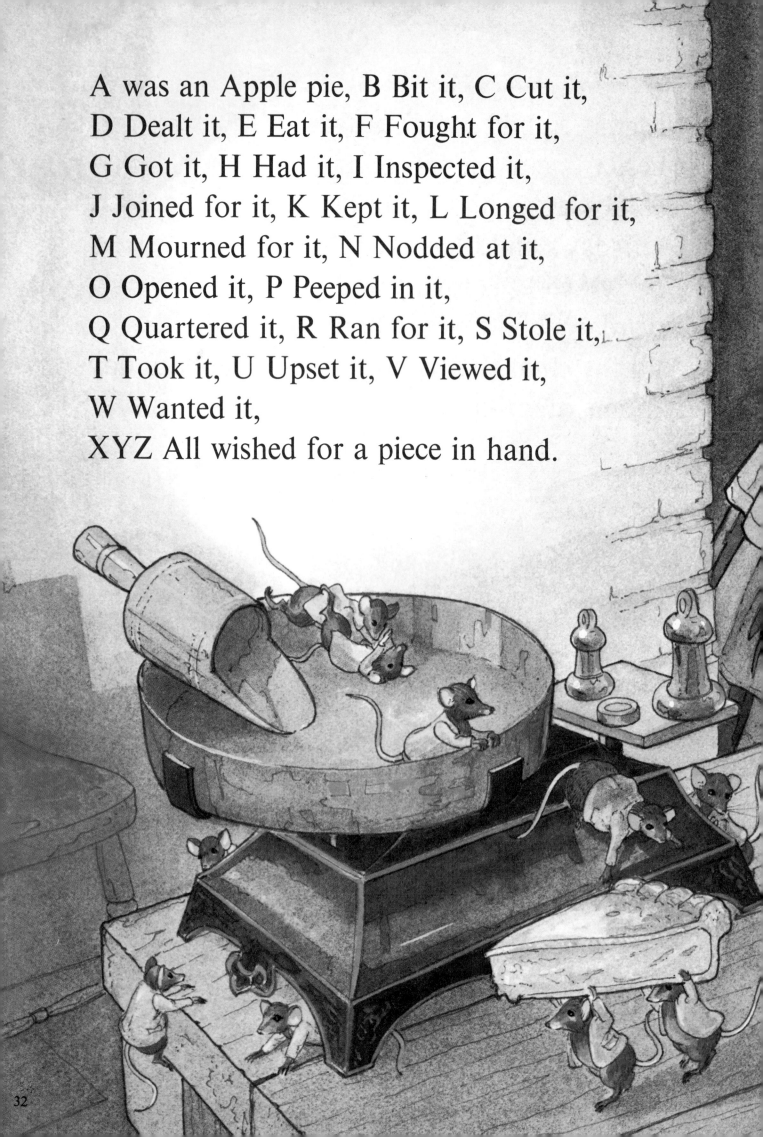

Solomon Grundy,
Born on a Monday,
Christened on Tuesday,
Married on Wednesday,
Took ill on Thursday,
Worse on Friday,
Died on Saturday,
Buried on Sunday.
This is the end
Of Solomon Grundy.

A, B, C, D, E, F, G,
Little Robin Redbreast sitting on a tree;
H, I, J, K, L, M, N,
He made love to little Jenny Wren;
O, P, Q, R, S, T, U,
Dear little Jenny, I want to marry you.
V, W, X, Y, Z,
Poor little Jenny she blushed quite red.

Anna Elise, she jumped with surprise;
The surprise was so quick, it played her a trick;
The trick was so rare, she jumped in a chair;
The chair was so frail, she jumped in a pail;
The pail was so wet, she jumped in a net;
The net was so small, she jumped on the ball;
The ball was so round, she jumped on the ground;
And ever since then she's been turning around.

My dame hath a lame tame crane,
My dame hath a crane that is lame.
Pray, gentle Jane, let my dame's lame tame crane
Feed and come home again.

This rhyme can be sung as a 'round'—a piece of music repeated by one or more voices, each entering before the previous voice has finished to produce an overlapping effect.

When the first voice reaches 2 a new voice enters singing the first line. When the latter reaches 2 another voice can enter singing the first line, and so on. The round can then be repeated at will.

My dame hath a lame tame crane,   My dame hath a crane that is lame.

Pray, gentle Jane, let my dame's lame tame crane Feed and come home a - gain.

Peter Piper picked a peck of pickled pepper;
A peck of pickled pepper Peter Piper picked;
If Peter Piper picked a peck of pickled pepper,
Where's the peck of pickled pepper
Peter Piper picked?

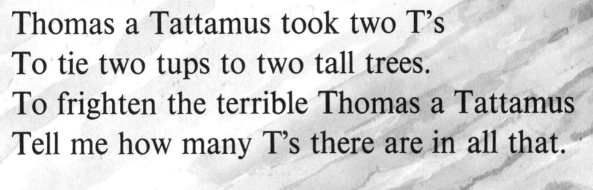

Thomas a Tattamus took two T's
To tie two tups to two tall trees.
To frighten the terrible Thomas a Tattamus
Tell me how many T's there are in all that.

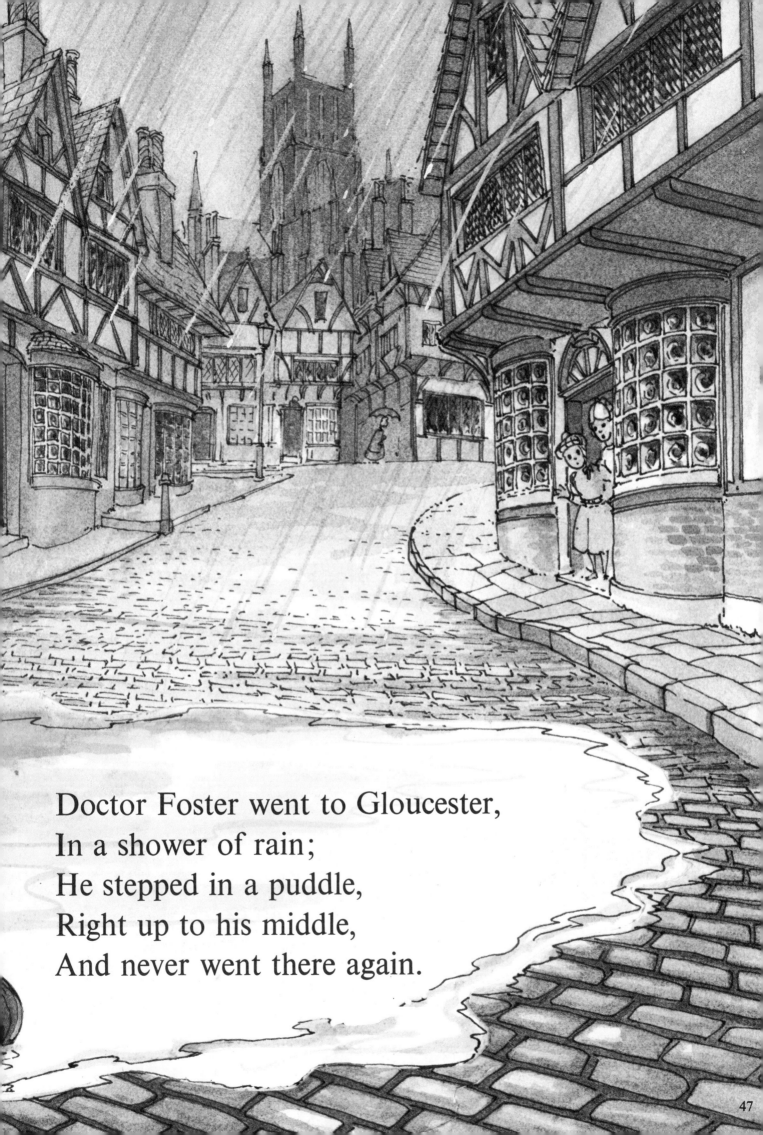

Doctor Foster went to Gloucester,
In a shower of rain;
He stepped in a puddle,
Right up to his middle,
And never went there again.

Old McDonald had a farm
E . . . I . . . E . . . I . . . O
And on that farm he had some cows,
E . . . I . . . E . . . I . . . O
With a moo-moo here,
And a moo-moo there,
Here a moo, there a moo,
Everywhere a moo-moo,
Old McDonald had a farm,
E . . . I . . . E . . . I . . . O

Old McDonald had a farm,
E . . . I . . . E . . . I . . . O
And on that farm he had some ducks,
E . . . I . . . E . . . I . . . O
With a quack-quack here, . . . *etc.*

. . *cats* . . mew-mew . . *dogs* . . woof-woof . .
. . *horses* . . neigh-neigh . . *lambs* . . baa-baa .

Old McDonald had a farm

Sing a song of sixpence,
A pocket full of rye;
Four and twenty blackbirds
Baked in a pie!
When the pie was opened
The birds began to sing;
Wasn't that a dainty dish
To set before the king?

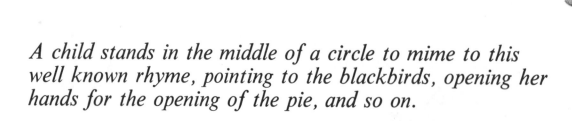

A child stands in the middle of a circle to mime to this well known rhyme, pointing to the blackbirds, opening her hands for the opening of the pie, and so on.

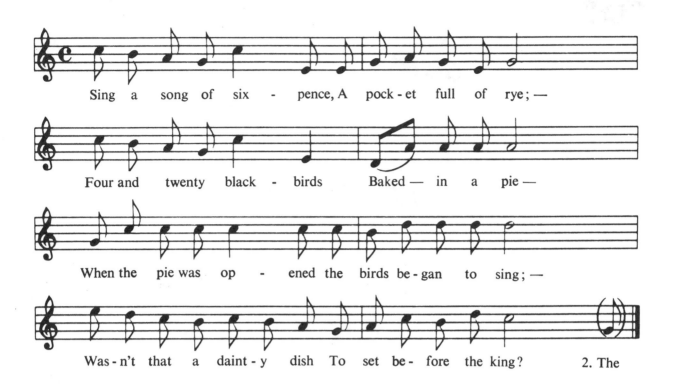

Sing a song of six - pence, A pock - et full of rye; —

Four and twenty black - birds Baked — in a pie —

When the pie was op — ened the birds be - gan to sing; —

Was - n't that a daint - y dish To set be - fore the king? 2. The

The king was in his counting house,
Counting out his money;

The queen was in the parlour,
Eating bread and honey.

The maid was in the garden,
Hanging out the clothes,

When down came a blackbird
And pecked off her nose.

I had a little nut-tree,
Nothing would it bear
But a silver nutmeg
And a golden pear;
The King of Spain's daughter
Came to visit me,
And all for the sake of my little nut-tree.
I skipped over water,
I danced over sea,
And all the birds in the air couldn't catch me

O, have you seen the muffin man,
The muffin man, the muffin man;
O, have you seen the muffin man
Who lives in Drury Lane O?

O yes, I've seen the muffin man,
The muffin man, the muffin man;
O yes, I've seen the muffin man
Who lives in Drury Lane O.

*Players join hands to form a ring.
One child is blindfolded and stands
in the centre with a stick or rolled
newspaper in his hand.*

*Everyone sings the QUESTION verse.
At the end the blindfolded player touches
someone in the ring. This person sings
the RESPONSE verse at the end of which
the blindfolded child guesses who it can be.*

*If correct, the two children change places and
the game can begin again.*

O, have you seen the muf-fin man, The muf-fin man, the muf-fin man; O,

have you seen the muf-fin man Who lives in Dru - ry Lane O?